Science Detectives

Dona Herweck Rice

Consultants

Sally Creel, Ed.D.
Curriculum Consultant

Leann Iacuone, M.A.T., NBCT, ATC
Riverside Unified School District

Jill Tobin
California Teacher of the Year
Semi-Finalist
Burbank Unified School District

Image Credits: Cover & p.1 BloomImage/Getty Images; p.9 (top) William Casey/agefotostock; pp.2, 8, 9, (center),15 (bottom right), 13, 16, 17 (left), 23 iStock; p.4 (left) CCI Archives/Science Source; p.5 (left) Jeremy Bishop/Science Source; p.4 (right) Royal Astronomical Society/Science Source; pp.6, 7 (top) St. Mary's Hospital Medical School/Science Source; pp.20–21 (illustrations) Chris Sabatino; all other images from Shutterstock.

Library of Congress Cataloging-in-Publication Data

Rice, Dona, author.
Science detectives / Dona Herweck Rice; consultants, Sally Creel, Ed.D. curriculum consultant, Leann Iacuone, M.A.T., NBCT, ATC Riverside Unified School District, Jill Tobin, California Teacher of the Year Semi-Finalist Burbank Unified School District.
pages cm
Audience: K to grade 3.
Includes index.
ISBN 978-1-4807-4574-2 (pbk.)
ISBN 978-1-4807-5064-7 (ebook)
1. Science—Juvenile literature.
2. Science—Experiments—Juvenile literature. I. Title.
Q163.R47 2015
507—dc23

2014013191

Teacher Created Materials
5301 Oceanus Drive
Huntington Beach, CA 92649-1030
http://www.tcmpub.com

ISBN 978-1-4807-4574-2

Printed in China 51497

Table of Contents

Let's Find Out!

Ancient Chinese scientists study a compass.

Ancient Babylonian scientists study the stars.

Scientists have been studying the world for a long time. But what they know so far is just a small part of all there is to know.

How can we learn more?

A scientist today studies a volcano.

What will future scientists study?

Scientists are like **detectives**. They find clues. They put them together to solve the case. They study with care and write every detail. They think and think some more. They test their ideas.

Sir Alexander Fleming observes bread mold.

Good Practices

Scientists follow good **practices**. This means they follow a careful way of doing things. They observe, test, and note everything they do.

note

test

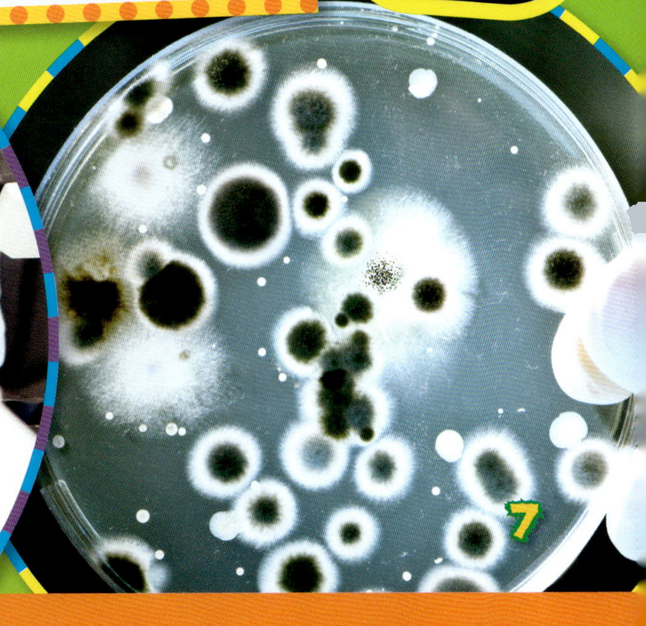

Tools of the Trade

To be a good detective, a scientist needs the right tools. There are tools for everything! But one tool is better than all the others. A scientist's brain is the most important "tool" there is!

What tools can we use?

A scientist writes his findings on paper.

Write It!

Something to write with is very important! Either paper or a computer will do. Then the scientist can record what he or she sees and does.

A scientist types her findings on a computer.

Magnify

Many tools are used to make things look bigger. They **magnify** them. A thing may be too small to see well. It may be too far away. A scientist needs help to see these things clearly.

Magnify It!

Here are some handy tools used to magnify things.

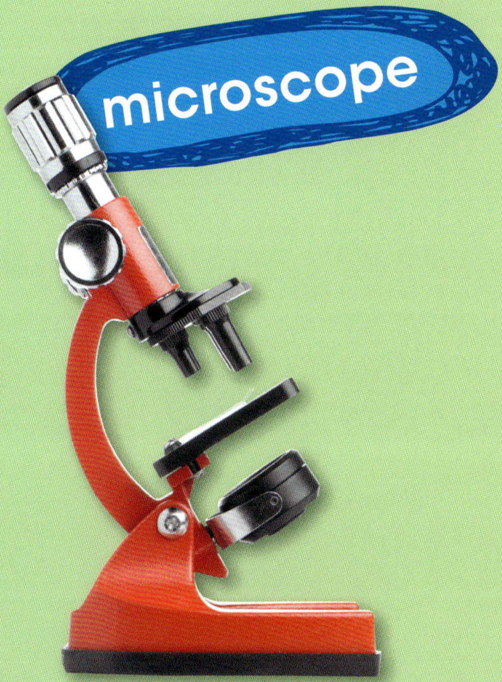

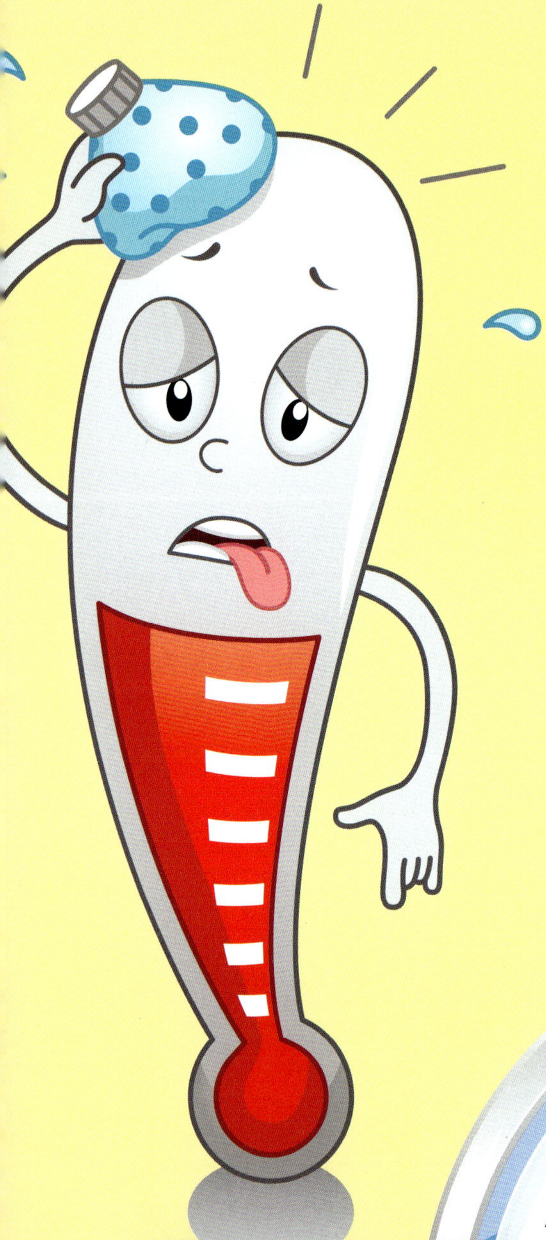

Gauge

Some tools can **gauge** (geyj) things. They measure it in some way. What does it weigh? How hot is it? There is a gauge for almost anything!

Gauge It!

Here are some handy tools used to gauge things.

thermometer

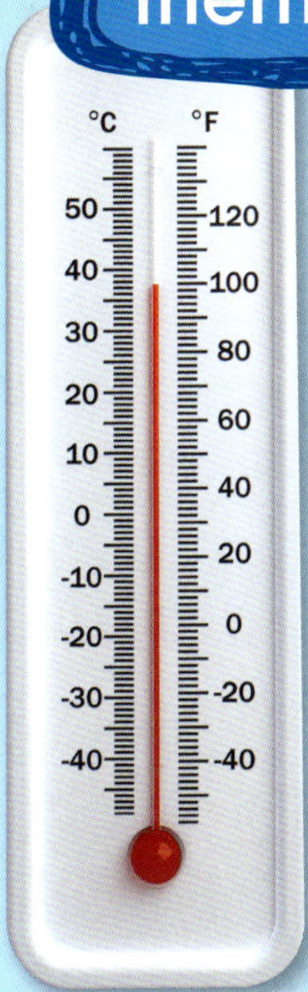

digital thermometer

scale

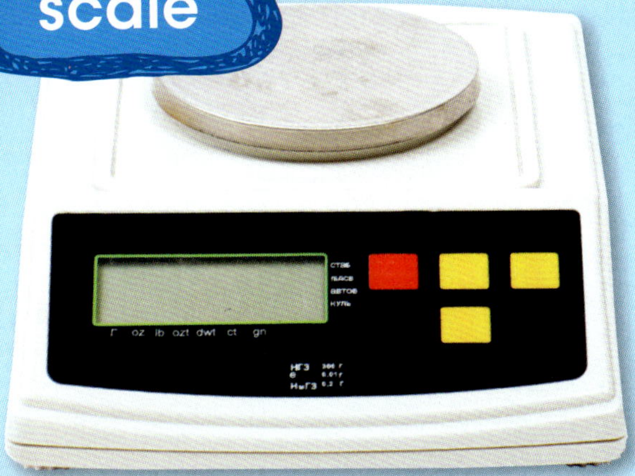

rain gauge

barometer

Break or Hold

A scientist may need to open a thing to look inside. Or, a scientist may need to hold a thing to study it better.

Break It!

Here are some handy tools to break or cut things apart.

Hold It!

Here are some handy tools to hold or contain things.

tweezers

petri dish

beakers

Protect

The first rule of science is to be careful! Science can be dangerous. A scientist must use care to be safe.

Warning!

Scientists often use **chemicals** (KEM-i-kuhlz). Chemicals may change things. They may be harmful if used without care.

Protect It!

Here are some handy tools to **protect** the scientist.

An Itch for Inquiry!

With the right tools, a scientist is ready to go. Well… *almost*. There is one more thing a scientist needs. It is an itch for inquiry! Like a good detective, a scientist stays on the case until there is an answer. Or until a new question pops up!

What's That?

To inquire is to think, study, and test. It is to dig and dig to get the answers and to follow each step with logic and care.

Let's Do Science!

What can you learn about water? Try this and see!

What to Get

- a few containers
- a freezer
- dirt
- water

What to Do

1. Pour water into different containers. What do you notice?

2. Pour water in dirt. What do you notice?

3. Put water in a freezer for a few hours. What do you notice?

4. Try some other ideas you have to learn about water. What else do you notice? Write what you observe.

Glossary

chemicals—things that may change the properties of other things

detectives—people who solve mysteries by studying clues

gauge—measure

magnify—make something appear bigger

practices—actions

protect—keep safe

Index

Your Turn!

I Want to Know!

Sit somewhere with a notebook and a pencil. Write everything you see, hear, and smell. Write what you would like to study.